ISBN 978-0-364-09891-2
PIBN 11337981

1 MONTH OF FREE READING

at
www.ForgottenBooks.com

By purchasing this book you are eligible for one month membership to ForgottenBooks.com, giving you unlimited access to our entire collection of over 1,000,000 titles via our web site and mobile apps.

To claim your free month visit:

www.forgottenbooks.com/free1337981

English
Français
Deutsche
Italiano
Español
Português

www.forgottenbooks.com

Mythology Photography **Fiction**
Fishing Christianity **Art** Cooking
Essays Buddhism Freemasonry
Medicine **Biology** Music **Ancient**
Egypt Evolution Carpentry Physics
Dance Geology **Mathematics** Fitness
Shakespeare **Folklore** Yoga Marketing
Confidence Immortality Biographies
Poetry **Psychology** Witchcraft
Electronics Chemistry History **Law**
Accounting **Philosophy** Anthropology
Alchemy Drama Quantum Mechanics
Atheism Sexual Health **Ancient History**
Entrepreneurship Languages Sport
Paleontology Needlework Islam
Metaphysics Investment Archaeology
Parenting Statistics Criminology
Motivational

Photo by Mathers, Middlesbrough

The Millennial Chorus

Singing Ambassadors of Goodwill

(See page 520)

TO MY SON

Do you know that your soul is of my soul
    such a part,
That you seem to be fibre and core of my
    heart?
None other can pain me as you, dear, can do;
None other can please me, or praise, as you.

Remember the world will be quick with its
    blame,
If shadow or stain ever darken your name,
"Like mother, like son," is a saying so true,
The world will judge largely of Mother by you.

Be this, then, your task, if task it should be,
To force the proud world to do homage to me.
Be sure it will say, when it's verdict you've
    won,
"She reaped as she sowed, lo, this is her son."

—Author Unknown to STAR

THE LATTER-DAY SAINTS'
MILLENNIAL STAR

ESTABLISHED IN 1840

No. 33, Vol. 100	Thursday, August 18, 1938	Price Two Pence

The MILLENNIAL STAR is published weekly by the British Mission of the Church of Jesus Christ of Latter-day Saints. Subscription price: 1s. 8d. for three months; 3s. 4d. for six months; and 6s. 6d. per year.

HUGH B. BROWN
Publisher
RICHARD R. LYMAN
Editor
MARVIN J. ASHTON
Associate-Editor

5 Gordon Square, London, W.C.1, England   Museum 1354

Thou believest that there is one God; thou doest well: the devils also believe, and tremble. But wilt thou know, O vain man, that faith without works is dead?—James 2: 19-20

CONTENTS

THIS WEEK'S COVER—

THE Millennial Chorus, travelling missionaries for the Church in Great Britain, are seen on the cover of this week's STAR. They include: front row, left to right, Richard P. Evans, A. Burt Keddington and J. Allen Jensen; second row, Aldon J. Anderson, William G. Woffinden, Richard B. Mendenhall, Mark P. Lyman, Ivan D. Voorhees, Walter D. Woffinden and Burton S. Miller; and third row, D. Maxwell Butler, William J. Seare, Philip L. Richards, Lowell M. Durham, John E. Gillespie, Jr. and Robert B. Buchanan.

The Holy Ghost

By Elder Charles A. Callis

Of the Council of the Twelve Apostles.

ON the sacred pages of the Book of Mormon these eternal truths appear: "Angels speak by the power of the Holy Ghost; wherefore, they speak the words of Christ." (II Nephi 32: 3) And again: "For when a man speaketh by the power of the Holy Ghost the power of the Holy Ghost carrieth it unto the hearts of the children of men." (II Nephi 33: 1)

A man is fearfully and wonderfully made. In this earthen vessel are heavenly treasures—an immortal spirit of which God is the Father, the immortal Priesthood and the immortal gift of the Holy Ghost. Surely we ought not to defile the temple of the Holy Ghost by using things which our Father hath forbidden. Quite recently one of the foremost captains of British industry visited Canada, and in the course of a public address gave this forceful admonition: "Do not think," he said, "that education weans you from the spiritual law." He was, of course, referring to education in a broad sense, to the schooling we receive in the University of Life. But when the spiritual law is subordinated to the selfish plans and feelings of men, misery steps in. If the spiritual law were dominant in the hearts of men there would be no wars. With few exceptions every war has been "a rich man's war and a poor man's fight." It is said that three-fourths of the men who fought in the Confederate Army never owned a slave.

President Brigham Young called Karl G. Maeser, the great educator, to go to Provo to organize and conduct an academy to be established in the name of the Church—a Church school. Before leaving for Provo to start his work he went to President Young and said: "Have you any instructions to give me?"

The President looked steadily forward for a few moments, as though in deep thought, then said: "Brother Maeser, I want you to remember that you ought not to teach even the alphabet or the multiplication tables without the Spirit of God. That is all. God bless you. Goodbye." That was Dr. Maeser's guiding star. By that spirit he reached the hearts and touched the lives of thousands for good and brought them into that true idealism—the right of the spiritual law to be uppermost in the hearts of men.

The work of the Holy Ghost is wonderful. The Prophet Joseph Smith said: "You might as well baptize a bag of sand as a man if not done in view of the remission of sins and getting of the Holy Ghost. Baptism by water is but half a baptism, and is good for nothing without the other half—that is, the baptism of the Holy Ghost." The regenerating and cleansing power of the Spirit is a blessing from heaven.

Jesus Christ tells us that "whatsoever ye would that men should do to you, do ye even so to them." We are told to rise above all carnal desires, to walk uprightly, conquering self, which will give us the testimony that we are pleasing God.

But how can men do these things without that greater power of righteousness in their souls that the Holy Ghost brings to them; that great regenerating force which enables them to cast from them lust, evil thoughts, and the thought of doing things that will hurt their fellow creatures? This great strength, the powerful operation of the Holy Ghost, will make one shake at the very appearance of evil.

There is another office of the Holy Ghost: He will guide into all truth. The Lord Jesus said: "Howbeit when he, the Spirit of truth, is come. he will guide you into all truth: for he shall not speak of himself; but whatsoever he shall hear, that shall he speak; and he will show you things to come. He shall glorify me; for he shall receive of mine, and shall shew it unto you."

And again He said: "But the Comforter, which is the Holy Ghost, whom the Father will send in my name, he shall teach

Elder Callis

you all things, and bring all things to your remembrance, whatsoever I have said unto you."

"He will guide you into all truth." What is truth? "And truth is knowledge of things as they are, and as they were, and as they are to come." What a broad, comprehensive definition of truth the Lord gives! And because we are guided into all truth by that infallible guide, the Comforter, we hold dear to our hearts these great fundamental principles: The divine parentage and the mission of the Lord Jesus Christ, His crucifixion and divine atonement, the glorious resurrection, eternal life, the eternity of the marriage covenant—all of which bring forth joys inexpressible, the unspeakable gifts of God, manifested to our souls by the Holy Spirit.

The Holy Ghost is an infallible witness that God is no respector of persons. All officers in the Church may have for their guidance and direction in the duties with which they are entrusted this blessed spirit of inspiration, so that they will hear behind them a voice, "This is the way, walk ye in it, when ye turn to the right or when ye turn to the left."

The Holy Ghost is the genius of the Holy Priesthood. Remove from the men of the Church, clothed with this power, dispossess them if that were possible of the guiding influence of the spirit of revelation and they would be as unproductive in the ministry as the dry sand on the seashore.

The Holy Ghost is the testimony of Jesus. "No man," said the Apostle Paul. "can say that Jesus is the Lord, but by the Holy Ghost." The Saviour declared that "the kingdom of God cometh not with observation," not by external show, for the world is deceived by outward ornament. "Man looketh on the outward appearance, but the Lord looketh on the heart."

When the Saviour of the world stood before that cruel judge, Pontius Pilate, and Pilate, in a sneering manner, addressed this question to the Saviour, "What is truth?" the embodiment of truth was before him. Truth personified was there. But Pontius Pilate could not recognize the truth. Why? Because "the kingdom of God cometh not with observation."

"Except a man be born again," said Jesus Christ, "he cannot see the kingdom of God," and "Except a man be born of water and of the Spirit, he cannot enter into the kingdom of God." It has been said by a philosopher, that the eye sees what the mind brings it the power to see.

The Latter-day Saints have the Holy Ghost in their hearts. John Wesley rose to a great height of inspiration when he said: "We through the Holy Ghost can witness better things." Because we have the gift of the Spirit we can behold all the wonderful truths of the Gospel. We know the kingdom of God is on the earth.

"Jesus asked his disciples, saying, Whom do men say that I the Son of man am? And they said, Some say that thou art John the Baptist: some, Elias; and others, Jeremias, or one of the prophets. He saith unto them, But whom say ye that I am? And Simon Peter answered and said, Thou art the Christ, the Son of the living God. And Jesus answered and said unto him, Blessed art thou, Simon Bar-jona: for flesh and blood hath not revealed it unto thee, but my Father which is in heaven. And I say also unto thee, That thou art Peter, and upon this rock I will build my church; and the gates of hell shall not prevail against it." (Matthew 16: 13-18)

I believe with all my heart and know that this Church is built upon the rock of revelation. Joseph Smith, an apostle of Jesus Christ, through whose instrumentality the Lord established His Church upon the earth for the last time, thus testifies of the resurrected Christ: "And now, after the many testimonies which have been given of Him, this is the testimony, last of all, which we give of Him; That he lives! For we saw him, even on the right hand of God; and we heard the voice bearing record that he is the Only Begotten of the Father."

DISTRICT CONFERENCES SCHEDULED

THE following dates have been announced for holding the Autumn Conferences throughout the Mission. Times and places of meetings will appear in subsequent issues of the STAR.

Newcastle	-	Sept. 4th	Liverpool -	Oct. 23rd
Scottish	-	Sept. 11th	Hull - - -	Oct. 30th
Welsh	- -	Sept. 18th	Sheffield -	Nov. 6th
Leeds	- -	Sept. 25th	Birmingham	Nov. 13th
Norwich	- -	Oct. 2nd	Bristol - -	Nov. 20th
Manchester		Oct. 9th	London - -	Nov. 27th
Nottingham		Oct. 16th		

The Soul's Fire

By JEREMIAH STOKES

THE Prophet began the publication of the *Times and Seasons* with the press and type that had been rescued from Far West. He organized the "Female Relief Society of Nauvoo," the purposes of which were, to aid the poor, nurse the sick and afflicted, and engage in general charitable work, and Emma Smith was chosen as its president. He completed the temple and introduced the sacred principles and ceremonies to be employed for the benefit of both the living and the dead.

He stressed more vigorously than ever the observance of the Word of Wisdom, a rule of health given to him by revelation eight or ten years before, which advised against the use of tea, coffee, tobacco, and strong drink. He launched a vigorous proselyting campaign and sent the apostles and many elders of the Church on local and foreign missions and dispatched Orson Hyde and John E. Page to Palestine to dedicate that land for the gathering of the Jews.

He turned the persecutions of Palmyra, the exodus from Kirtland, the extermination from Missouri, into a mighty force that entered a frontier wilderness and built the foremost commonwealth in the state of Illinois, a city of twenty thousand souls, a population that was only part of his vast organization that reached out into the states of the Union, into Canada, and across the sea.

Begin Story Here

DESPITE persecution suffered by the Church, missionaries were continually being sent throughout the States, and to Great Britain. Ann Northrop, an English woman, is impressed by the Gospel message, but a prejudiced husband forbids her associating with its people. In Missouri, by the Governor's order, the Mormons are driven from the State and move to Quincy, Illinois. Joseph Smith and other leaders, held six months without trial, are finally released and join their families. The people move to Nauvoo, Illinois, set up a thriving city, and a new era seems dawning for the Church.

But, while the growing tree of progress was putting forth its green leaves and bright blossoms of promise, insidious cankerworms of jealousy and hate were boring at the roots, destroyers that came both from within the fold as well as from without.

The far-flung proselyting net of the new faith had gathered fish of all kind, genuinely sound for the most part, but not altogether free from the loathsome catch which is akin to the scuttle fish that leaves a trail of blinding slime along its course and the sword fish that stabs and kills. And so within the tent were those impelled by motives of treachery as well as

(Continued on page 522)

Science and Religion

By Elder Nephi Jensen

THERE are four great constructive agencies in the world today—science, philosophy, art and religion. A correct understanding of the distinctive task of each of these instrumentalities of civilization will do much to dispel the supposed conflict between science and religion.

What is the distinctive task of each of these agencies? A very simple illustration will aid us in finding the right answer to this vital question. You have in your pocket a little machine. It is round in shape and rather flat. On one side there is a dial, with moving hands that mark time, or time intervals. You can approach this little machine from four distinct angles.

Suppose the watch should stop running. You would immediately be confronted with a problem—the problem of finding out just why the watch had stopped going. That is a problem in science. It is a very simple task to be sure. If a technician in watch making should examine the watch and determine just why it had stopped, and do no more, he would have performed a purely scientific task. For it is the distinctive task of science to find the facts and discover the truth. If this watch technician were disposed to act like a real scientist, and you should ask him to repair your watch, he would promptly say, "I do not repair watches. I am a scientist. I simply find the facts."

Now suppose you should become interested in the precise function of your watch in its relationship to the sum total of truth; and should want to know the relation of the element of time, or time measurement, to the totality of truth, you would be confronted with a problem in philosophy. For it is the task of philosophy to systematize and unify truth. If you should desire to solve this problem you would call to your assistance a philosopher. For the philosopher is a unifier of truth.

Suppose you should become dissatisfied with the ornamentation on your watch case. You would then be confronted with a task in art. For it is the distinctive task of art to create the beautiful; and to put a robe of beauty on things to signify that they are complete.

Finally suppose your watch should stop running because the mainspring had lost its elasticity; and you should touch the spring with some energizing substance and re-sensitize it. You would be performing a task analogous to the task of religion. For it is the distinctive mission of religion to touch the mainspring of the soul—the conscience—and awaken it to new life, energy and power.

Or, substituting truth for the watch: it is the special mission of science to discover truth; it is the special mission of philosophy to unify and systematize truth; it is the special mission of art to put a robe of beauty on the truth; and it is the distinctive mission of religion to kindle in the heart a love for the truth.

More than any other religion in the world, Mormonism fulfils this high mission of religion. By its new revelations of God's purposes regarding the establishment of His Kingdom in the world, it intensifies faith in God and awakens the deathless love for truth that leads to the glorification of the beautiful, the good, and the true.

*B*rowsings in Brief . . .

y
P
r
e
s
i
d
e
n
t

H
u
g
h

B.

B
r
o
w
n

COMMON sense said, let him suffer, firmly let the
    black ox tread.
Grace said, if he comes, I'll give welcome, aye,
    with board and bed.
Long stood Kindness in the doorway hoping he
    might chance to pass.
Love went after him to worlds end, bare foot, over
    broken glass.

                      —Fay Inchfawn

*   *   *

PRIZE not thyself by what thou hast, but by what thou art; he that values a jewel by its golden frame, or a book by its silver clasp, or a man by his vast estates, errs.—Quarles

*   *   *

WHENEVER nature leaves a hole in a person's mind, she generally plasters it over with a thick coat of self-conceit.—Longfellow

*   *   *

OLDER men seem somehow to live in the afterglow of faith. Men at large need the sunrise.

THE idea of philosophy is truth; the idea of religion is life.

PHILOSOPHY superficially studied excites doubt; When thoroughly explored, dispels it.—Bacon

*   *   *

CREEDS grow so thick along the way their boughs hide God.—Reese

*   *   *

RELIGION, if it be true, is central truth, and all knowledge which is not gathered round it and quickened and illuminated by it is hardly worth the name.—Channing

THURSDAY, AUGUST 18, 1938

EDITORIAL

Singing Ambassadors

SIXTEEN strong, the Millennial Chorus, a group of young Mormon missionaries representing the Church of Jesus Christ of Latter-day Saints, is singing its way into the hearts of countless Britishers. Decked in dressy white jackets and dark trousers, the songsters have been and are appearing night and day before the general public. Thousands of cinema visitors have become acquainted with "The Millennial Chorus from Salt Lake City, Utah."

For the past few months the Chorus has been filling a circuit to various cinema theatres throughout Great Britain. After performing for approximately one week in a town or city the group then moves on to the next appointment. Through their past performances and behaviour their reputation goes before them and in every case they have been and are being well received by promoters all over Britain.

Thousands Of New Contacts

ONE can imagine the number of people that are coming into contact with these Mormon missionaries when he stops to calculate the number of attenders at a given show-house during a week. With two or three performances each day for one week before audiences of up to two and three thousand each session it is not over estimating to say that in one week more than 25,000 people are coming into contact with these singing ambassadors during their cinema circuit. One appreciates still more the work of this group when he pauses to recall that for more than three months this type of activity has been taking place. Thousands, the large majority for the first time, have come in contact with Mormon missionaries.

Through this method of spreading Mormon goodwill one-time prejudiced individuals are now seeing Mormons in a different light. Spectators pleased with the performance of the Chorus only have to ask, to have the group fill engagements for them in private groups or social units. Through their willingness to be of service and their voluntary performances they are extremely popular. Autograph seekers and Millennial Chorus "fans" are not uncommon in the communities where the sixteen elders sing.

Return Performances Sought

NEGRO spirituals, sociability and novelty numbers are presented as selections for the audience's entertainment. So pleased have been the general public and the managers of the theatres with the singing and popularity of the Millennial Chorus that numerous return engagements have been asked for.

A collection of newspaper clippings from the various places where the group has performed clearly indicates the feeling of the public toward the Mormon elders, who teach their doctrines principally by song and conduct. Pictures and oftentimes lengthy articles herald the Chorus's ability, and speak of the purpose and nature of their missionary work.

During the day, when the Chorus is not filling engage- ments, the members tract in the district in which they are performing. Very often they are greeted at the door with the statement, "Yes, I know who you are. I heard you at the cinema last evening." Friends have been made through the singing of the group and further interest in the message of the missionaries is shown when the people know who they are.

Invited To Conduct Services

SCHOOLS, clubs, adult classes, hospitals, churches and various other organizations are visited by the group. Again more contacts for the Church are made. Often times the songsters have been invited to conduct services in various churches and chapels. Here they furnish appropriate music and deliver sermons on the Gospel as taught by the Church. No matter what the creed or religion of the people they appear before might be, they cannot help but admire the views and the con- duct of this outstanding group of young men. Their mission of unselfishness and love cannot be over-looked by the most critical eye.

There is not a more effective means of making friends for the Church in Britain than through the efforts of the mem- bers of the Millennial Chorus. Friends are being made in each town and city in which they stop. Where once the door was closed to Mormonism, today it is open and bids the elders welcome.

Firmly believing and advocating the statement of Christ, "Go ye into all the world and preach the gospel to every creature," this group willingly carries the message of "peace on earth, goodwill to men." Through the medium of song this organization hopes to contact thousands and by their work and actions lead people to an investigation of the message they are in possession of.

A. Burt Keddington, Conductor

UNDER the able direction of their conductor, Elder A. Burt Keddington, an active member for more than two years, the Chorus has gone forward with unmeasured effectiveness. Labouring hand in hand as a unit with a single purpose the brotherhood and friendship found within the ranks is beyond reproach. Members of the Chorus are: Elders Keddington, Aldon J. Anderson, group president, Richard P. Evans, J. Allen Jensen, Walter D. Woffinden, Richard B. Mendenhall, Mark P. Lyman, Ivan D. Voorhees, William G. Woffinden, Burton S. Miller, D. Maxwell Butler, William J. Seare, Philip L. Richards, Lowell M. Durham, John E. Gillespie, Jr. and Robert B. Buchanan.

They are indeed singing ambassadors of goodwill and a credit to the Church they represent.—MARVIN J. ASHTON

THE SOUL'S FIRE
(Continued from page 517)

(Continued from page 517)

those who were actuated by sincerity of heart, loyalty to the Prophet, and devotion to the Cause.

Christmas eve rolled around and the Prophet and Hyrum and a host of friends had gathered at the former's home to celebrate his release from the charges implicating him in Missouri. Music and dancing among church officials, relatives and intimate friends were engaging the time and attention of all who were present.

Suddenly, the door was thrown open, and a poorly clad man with long hair stood inside.

"Porter Rockwell!" exclaimed the Prophet rushing towards him and embracing him. "How did you get away from Missouri? You're cold, and I know you're hungry, Come, be warmed and fed, and then you may answer my question."

When Porter had eaten, he returned to the festive room. The Prophet took the best chair at his command and set it near the fire place, that his friend might feel the warmth of the burning logs.

"And now for your story, Porter. We're all anxious to hear it," said the Prophet.

The man slowly arose to respond to the request.

"I went to the states," he began, "to New Jersey; and when the Prophet was discharged, I started home. At St. Louis, some-one recognized me and I was arrested. They chained my hands and brought me to Independence. My bond was fixed at four thousand dollars and only Missouri property holders could qualify. I could not get bail and so I was kept in prison. Once I escaped, but was recaptured. When I was brought back, a mob gathered and wanted to hang me. Later they gave me a hearing for breaking jail, and the judge set me free, but they kept me in jail for safe keeping until, well, here I am, Joseph, ready to continue my service for you and the Cause I love."

As the party was breaking up, Porter called the Prophet aside and said, "Joseph, I don't want to upset your mind, but I must tell you that the Missourians are still going to try to get you on the old charges made at Gallatin. The deputy jailer at Independence so informed me, and from what the sheriff told me, I know someone here, someone you do not suspect, is betraying you into their hands. Letters are being sent to them from Nauvoo, I saw the writing, but not the names. The sheriff showed it to me."

"I want you to stay with me for the night, Porter. We'll discuss the matter further after the folks are gone."

After the guests left, Joseph and Porter went into conference.

As their interview ended, the Prophet said, "Porter, I suspect my first counsellor, William Law, of treachery. His spirit is not the same. He was not here tonight, and I don't trust him. He has kept away from me for months. Will you contact William and find out if I am right or wrong in my suspicions?"

"Yes, Joseph, I'll get an interview early in the morning."

Next morning, as William Law sat in his home, he heard a knock at the door.

"Come in," he called, and Porter Rockwell entered.

"Well, Porter, when did you get back? Quite a stranger. Come in," said Law, taking his hand and giving it a friendly grip. "Have a chair. Let's see, you've been gone several months, haven't you?"

"Yes, William, about eight of 'em. And tough months they've been, too, I'll tell you. I've had just about all of this kind of religion I want. I've been in jail long enough to think it over, and I'm beginning to feel that it ain't worth the candle. Things don't pan out like Joseph said they should."

"Beginning to get a little dissatisfied, eh, Porter?" rejoined Mr. Law, cheerfully.

"It's more than little dissatisfied, William."

"Not thinking of quitting Joseph, are you, Porter?"

"If I thought there were enough of the same turn of mind,

From an old engraving of Nauvoo

I'm quite certain I would," he replied, taking his knife from his pocket, cutting off a splinter from a stick of wood and beginning to whittle.

"There are plenty of us in that frame of mind, Porter," volunteered the man, lowering his voice to a confidential pitch, "a lot of us just like you, men who feel that Joseph is a fallen prophet and that he must be removed to save the Church."

"I don't know but that you're right, William," Rockwell drawled, seriously. "I talked with the sheriff at Independence about this very matter, and he's ready to join us on any plan that we might think up to get rid of Joseph, at least I think he is, if I am not mistaken in the man. He made me an offer to trick Joseph into his hands and I refused. I've been thinking it over lately and half regret that I didn't take him up on it. I would see him again, if I could make him believe I was 'on the level'."

"I can fix that Porter, easy enough. I know the sheriff; in fact I'm in touch with him. I'll give you a note telling him you're with us and that will take care of everything."

That evening, after dark, Porter went back to the Prophet. "You had better pull down the blinds, Joseph," he said. "It's dangerous for us to be seen together."

"There," said the Prophet, as he blew out the candle. "That's much safer."

The two men sat down together.

"I saw William this morning, Joseph," Porter began, "and had quite a talk with him. He gave me a note to the sheriff at Independence. Here it is."

He took the sheet from his pocket and gave it to Joseph.

"That note is in exactly the same handwriting as a letter that the sheriff at Independence showed me. William Law is the traitor. He is the fellow who is in communication with the sheriff. He's one of the gang who is working to overthrow you. I got it from his own lips."

Joseph Smith

Just then the door opened, and Emma came into the room.

"Joseph," she said, "Emer Harris is here and wants to see you. He says it is very important, and he can't wait."

Joseph motioned to Porter to step into the bedroom as he himself went to receive the caller.

"Good evening, President Smith," said the man. "I want to see you privately."

"Step in," said the Prophet, taking a candle and pointing the way to the room that he and Rockwell had just occupied together. "Be seated, Brother Harris."

The man sat down and at once started his errand.

"Brother Smith, it is a very important question I want to ask you. You see, my boy Denison and Robert Scott, who live with William Law, have been invited to go to a meeting that's being held tonight by some of the apostates, and the boys say I am invited to go along, too. I don't know what to do about it and thought I'd better come to you for advice."

"I think you ought to stay away, Emer, but I advise the boys to go. Tell them to come over to see me before they leave. Will you do that?"

"Yes, indeed I will, President Smith. The boys are at my house right now. I'll go and fetch them at once. I'll only be a few minutes."

"Did you hear what Brother Harris said?" asked the Prophet. "I intended you should."

"Yes," replied Rockwell.

(To be continued next week)

Talks on Doctrine

By ELDER MATTHIAS F. COWLEY

MARRIAGE

NO people hold more sacred the principle of marriage, nor esteem more highly the possession of chastity than do the Latter-day Saints. Among no people is a lapse of virtue so rare as among this people. We consider sexual crime the most blighting curse that infests the earth today. Adultery is considered as next to murder in the catalogue of crime. Individuals guilty of fornication or adultery are promptly excommunicated from the Church unless the sin is followed by the most profound repentance and the best restitution which can possibly be made.

The children around the family altar, in Sunday School, Mutual Improvement Associations, Primary Associations, and all the institutions of the Church are taught to hold their virtue more sacred to them than life itself. When they attain the years of maturity and enter the holy state of matrimony they vow before God, angels, and living witnesses that they will never violate the marriage covenant. We believe that God ordained the union of the sexes in marriage not only for time but for all eternity.

It is largely due to this fact and to the deeply religious elements which enter into marriage among our people that divorces are so rare. Young men and women are taught that while pure love and perfect congeniality should exist between the parties to the marriage covenants, passion and infatuation should not be the ruling motive, but principle should control; and that in the weakness of humanity the dangers of mistakes in the mating of sexes are so great that the only safe way is to seek in prayer and supplication the guidance of divine providence. They are also taught to so live in daily walk and conversation that their heavenly Father will answer their prayers.

To feel sublimely impressed that marriage is for eternity and that God is directly interested in us tends to make our people more careful and considerate, more prayerful, in choosing of husband or wife than they otherwise would be. To increase the solemnity of the ceremony God has commanded that the work should be performed in a holy temple erected to His name. The result of such teaching is a far greater percentage of happy unions and a much smaller percentage of divorces among the Latter-day Saints than among other communities.

That marriages should be for all eternity is evident from holy writ. When Adam and Eve were married there was no death and hence the union would endure forever. We are told by Isaiah that God will annul their covenant with death. In the book of Ecclesiastes it is written, "I know that whatsoever God doeth it shall be forever."

News of Current Interest

POLITICAL promises, the butt of countless jokes and cynicisms, may become obsolete in Canada if proposed laws are passed. Briefly, it is planned to make it an offence for a candidate to sign a questionnaire or pledge binding himself to any specific course of action, or promising to promote the expenditure of public money on behalf of any person, group of persons, or organization.

MANCHESTER has reason to believe that it has provided its share of famed British personages. David Lloyd George, Sir John Simon, and Richard Cobden are three of the statesmen who were born, or lived there. Authors include Thomas de Quincy, John Byron, Harrison Ainsworth, Mrs. Gaskell and Louis Golding. John Alcock, who was on the first plane to cross the Atlantic, and William Boyd Dawkins, a leading geologist of last century, both came from Manchester. Charles Halle, the musician, and Thomas Wright, who started a national fund to aid discharged prisoners, were two other Manchester citizens.

RUBBER surfaced roads, used at present, because of the cost, only in vicinity of churches, hospitals, schools and similar places where silence is essential, may become more widely used in the future due to the decreasing cost of rubber, and reports that longer wear, less vibration and shock absorbing qualities tend to over-rule higher initial outlay.

BRINGING a lake into the classroom did not appeal to the professors of the Genesco Normal School at Rochester, New York, as being practical. Instead students were sent, equipped with diving helmets, to the bottom of the lake where they studied the fauna and flora in its own environment. Other modern equipment includes a two-way radio set which enables students in the field to describe various insects and plants to those in the classroom. Next year the college hopes to have radio discussions from the bottom of the lake.

CABBAGE-TREE hats, kangaroo-skin overcoats and calfskin waistcoats, proud possessions of old-time Australian bushmen, have almost disappeared from ordinary view, and have taken with them much of the colour of the former-day street crowds. In olden times a backwoodsman in for his yearly process of "going to town" could be picked out a block away, but younger natives prefer to dress as nearly like ordinary city folk as possible, perhaps as protective colouration.

SEALED CABINS are expected to solve the problem of passenger comfort at flying altitudes of 40,000 feet or more. These cabins carry their own atmosphere and pressure, and are unaffected by outside conditions. Compressed oxygen is carried and released into the cabin as needed. Recent successful tests in America indicate that a regular 10 hour schedule between New York and Los Angeles, a distance of over 3,000 miles, will be made practical by using the sub-stratosphere—30,000 to 40,000 feet up—as the path of the plain.

RICE three times a day is the usual Japanese menu. Fish, beans, vegetables, pickles, and seaweed are other items, but rice remains the outstanding dish, and has a percapita consumption of over five bushels per year.

WATER DRIPPING upon a stone will wear it away during the course of many years. By a special arrangement of a flywheel whose edge moves at 13 miles a minute—twice as fast as a rifle bullet—steel is tested by having water, at ordinary tap pressure, turned upon it. Due to the impact caused by the terrific speed of the wheel, even the toughest alloys can be cut through in a few minutes.

CHOICE of fresh or salt water is offered to captains docking at Vancouver, British Columbia. The main harbour contains salt, but boats long at sea, and needing barnacles scraped off the hull, may be driven around the point and up the Fraser estuary to fresh water.

BACHELORS, already subject to heavy taxation in Italy, were given another set-back by a recent decree preventing them, along with widowers who have no children, from holding the post of Mayor, or similar high public office. Those now in office must resign.

News of the Church in the World

STATING that "No movement of peoples was ever more entitled to recognition than that made by the Mormons from Nauvoo, Illinois, to the Great Salt Lake Valley," Ralph Budd, president of the Burlington Railroad in the United States, promised Utahns that Nauvoo is to be restored as a public interest centre. The city will be set apart as a state park, and attempts will be made to restore the site as it was when the Mormons lived there. The work is expected to be well under way by 1939, the time of the Nauvoo centenary, which will attract hosts of people back to the historic town.

SIXTY-EIGHTH annual convention of the American Society of Civil Engineers was held recently in Salt Lake City, Utah. Five hundred official delegates from all parts of the nation gathered to hear their leaders discuss and present problems pertaining to their work. Scheduled on the programme were visits to early historic sites of the state, and various engineering accomplishments found near Salt Lake City. Among the papers read before the groups, which received interesting comment, was one dealing with the Lyman system of street numbering, written by President Richard R. Lyman, which undertakes to solve the problem of effectively systematizing house addresses in any city.

From the Mission Field

Departing Missionaries—

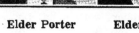

Elder Porter   Elder Blanch

Elder Arthur C. Porter, who has laboured in Norwich District, as Associate-Editor of the MILLENNIAL STAR, and as superintendent of Mission Sunday Schools, was honourably released on Wednesday, August 10th, and will return to his home in Rexburg, Idaho.

Elder Grant E. Blanch, who has laboured in Newcastle District, and London District, was honourably released on Wednesday, August 10th, and will return to his home in Ogden, Utah.

Appointments—
Elder Daniel Garn Heaton was appointed supervising elder of Hull District on Thursday, August 4th.

Elder A. Ferron Forsgren was appointed European Mission secretary on Wednesday. August 10th.

Transfers—
Elder Dale W. Ansell was transferred from Sheffield District to Bristol District, on Thursday, August 4th.

Elder Charles W. Hailes was transferred from Hull District to Nottingham District on Thursday, August 4th.

Doings in the Districts—

HULL—On Friday, July 29th, the Relief Society of Hull Branch sponsored a pie supper. Special guests of the evening were Sisters Nellie Hailes, and her daughter Irene, mother and sister of Elder Charles W. Hailes, who are visiting here in Britain. Sister Amelia M. Ranson and her counsellors directed the games and programme.

Sisters Aloa Dixon and Anna Saunders directed community singing and games at a social held in Hull Branch, Thursday, August 4th. Ice cream and cakes were served to the group during the latter part of the evening.

On Saturday, August 6th, the M.I.A. held an outing at Hornsea, travelling there by bus and cycle. Games on the sands and swimming in the ocean, followed by lunch, constituted the day's programme.

Gainsborough Branch held its annual outing at Cleethorpe on Saturday, July 23rd, with approximately 50 in attendance. The entire day was spent in various games and activities enjoyed by all.

LIVERPOOL—Wigan Branch held its annual open air service at the branch camp at Blackpool, on the evening of Sunday, July 31st. Brother Benjamin Burchall and Supervising Elder E. Max Phillips were the speakers. Brother Horace E. Heyes presided over the meeting, which was attended by over 50 people from various branches including Preston and Nuneaton.

NEWCASTLE—A social was given at Skelton Branch honouring Mr. George R. Clarke and Sister Rose Eleanor Rudd, who were recently married. Supervising Elder George S. Walker read over the marriage ceremony and a duet was sung by Sisters Kathleen Featherstrong and Nellie Rudd. A reception followed immediately after the programme.

On Sunday, July 31st, the Middlesbrough Branch presidency was reorganized. The brethren released, after many years' service, are James Thompson, president; Christopher Bushey, first counsellor; and Richard Harland, second counsellor. The new presidency sustained by the Branch are J. Albert Pennock, president, and Brothers Thompson and Harland, first and second counsellors, respectively.

West Hartlepool and Middlesbrough combined in a Bank Holiday outing to Middleton-on-Row, which was sponsored by the former. Games and hiking were the principal activities.

A social was held by members of the Carlisle Branch on Saturday, July 30th. Sister Lillian Wallace had charge of general arrangements, and Elder Leslie W. Dunn directed the programme. On August 1st, the M.I.A. went on a ramble to "The Gills." Cricket, rounders and refreshments were the chief diversions. Sisters Wallace and Winifred Gill made all arrangements.

NOTTINGHAM—The Rochdale Greys, who recently won the national baseball championship, and the Sheffield Dons, another all-Mormon team, played an exhibition game in Hucknall in connection with the city's carnival activities recently. Approximately 1,000 people were in attendance to watch the game and listen to Elder Paul Howells describe the plays, explain who the teams were and their purpose here. Following the game a social was given in the Branch Hall for those saints who had come to see the game.

On August 1st, Nottingham Branch held an outing at Woolston Park. Games and community singing, followed by refreshments, were the activities.

SHEFFIELD — Sheffield and Rawmarsh Branch M.I.A. organizations, with three visitors from Barnsley, conducted a swimming party at Rotherham Baths recently. On July 26th, a farewell social in honour of Sister Florence Malmberg, who has been honourably released, was held at the home of President Joseph Thomas Quinney. Sister Elsie May Quinney presented Sister Malmberg with a hat box as a token of esteem from the members of the branch.

WELSH—Merthyr Tydfil Branch M.I.A. sponsored a social on Thursday, July 28th. Approximately 75 people gathered to participate in the dancing. The proceeds will be used for the Sunday School outing.

LATTER-DAY SAINT MEETING PLACES IN BRITAIN

(All meetings begin at 6.30 Sunday evenings unless otherwise indicated.)

Aberdeen:
Corn Exchange,
Hadden Street,
Off Market Street.

Accrington:
*L. D. S. Hall,
Over 9, Church St.

Airdrie:
‡L. D. S. Hall,
40, Hallcraig Street.

Barnsley:
Arcade Buildings.

Batley:
*L. D. S. Hall,
13, Wellington Street.

Belfast:
†Arcade Buildings,
122, Upper North St.

Birmingham:
L. D. S. Chapel,
23, Booth Street.
Handsworth.
Council Schools,
Stratford Road,
Sparkbrook.

Blackburn:
L. D. S. Hall,
St. Peter's Street.

Bolton:
Corporation
Chambers.

Bradford:
L. D. S. Chapel,
Woodlands Street,
Off City Road.

Brighton:
105, Queen's Road.

Bristol:
Hannah More Hall,
45, Park St., Clifton.

Burnley:
§L. D. S. Chapel,
1, Liverpool Road,
Rosegrove.

Carlisle:
L. D. S. Hall,
Scotch Street.

Cheltenham-Stroud:
Theosophical Hall,
St. Margaret's Ter.,
Off North Place,
Cheltenham.

Clayton:
*Central Hall.

Derby:
Unity Hall.

Doncaster:
*L. D. S. Hall,
Trafford Street.

Dublin:
†L. D. S. Hall,
8, Merrion Row.

Eastwood:
Library, Church St.

Edinburgh:
Ruskin House,
15, Windsor Street.

Gainsborough:
*L. D. S. Hall,
Curtis Yard.

Gateshead:
Westfield Hall,
Westfield Terrace.

Glasgow:
L. D. S. Hall,
4, Nelson Street.

Gravesend:
Freeborn Hall,
Peacock Street.

Great Yarmouth:
L. D. S. Hall,
33a, Regent Street.

Grimsby:
Thrift Hall,
Pasture Street.

Halifax:
*L. D. S. Hall,
35, Brinton Terrace,
Off Hansen Lane.

Hucknall:
*Byron Buildings.

Hull:
L. D. S. Chapel,
Wellington Lane, and
Berkeley Street.

Hyde:
L. D. S. Hall,
Reynolds Street.

Kidderminster:
L. D. S. Chapel,
Park Street.

Leeds:
*L. D. S. Hall,
5, Westfield Road.

Leicester:
All Saints' Open,
Great Central Street.

Letchworth:
Vasanta Hall,
Gernon Walk.

Liverpool:
L. D. S. Chapel,
301, Edge Lane.

London:
L. D. S. Chapel,
59, Clissold Rd., N.16.
Ravenslea Chapel,
149, Nightingale Lane
S.W.12.
Downham Fellowship
Club, between 29 & 30,
Arcus Rd., off Glenbow
Rd., Catford.
Ivy Hall,
Wellesley Road,
Gunnersbury, W.4.

Loughborough:
Adult School.

Lowestoft:
L. D. S. Hall,
20, Clapham Road.

Luton:
Dallow Road Hall.
Corner of Dallow and
Naseby Roads.

Mansfield:
39a, Albert Street.

Manchester:
L. D. S. Hall,
88, Clarendon Road.
C. on M.

Merthyr Tydfil:
L. D. S. Chapel,
Penyard Road.

Middlesbrough:
L. D. S. Hall,
188, Linthorpe Road.

Nelson:
*L. D. S. Hall,
10, Hibson Road.

Northampton:
*L. D. S. Chapel,
89, St. Michael's Str.

Nottingham:
L. D. S. Hall,
8, Southwell Road.

Norwich:
L. D. S. Chapel,
60, Park Lane.

Nuneaton:
Masonic Hall.

Oldham:
L. D. S. Hall,
Neville Street.

Plymouth:
L. D. S. Hall,
34, Park Street,
Tavistock Road.

Pontllanfraith:
Enquire:
81, Brynteg Street.

Preston, Lancs:
L. D. S. Hall,
7, Lords Walk,
Off North Road.

Rawmarsh:
L. D. S. Hall,
Main Street.

Rochdale:
L. D. S. Chapel,
Lower Sheriff St.

Sheffield:
L. D. S. Chapel,
Corner of Ellesmere
and Lyons Roads.

Shildon:
*L. D. S. Hall,
100, Main Street.

Skelton:
*14, Olliver Street,
Redcar, Yorks.

South Shields:
L. D. S. Chapel,
98, Fowler Street.

St. Albans:
49, Spencer Street.

Sunderland:
L. D. S. Chapel,
18, Tunstall Road.

Tipton, Wolverhampton:
L. D. S. Hall,
Washington Building,
Berry Street.

Varteg:
Memorial Hall.

West Hartlepool:
L. D. S. Chapel,
7, Osborne Road.

Wigan:
*L and Y Station.

§—6.15 p.m.   *—6.00 p.m   †—7.00 p.m.   ‡—2.30 p.m.

CPSIA information can be obtained
at www.ICGtesting.com
Printed in the USA
BVHW090639211118
533509BV00031BA/4429/P